Edmonton Travel Guide

What You Need to See and Do

By Michael Persaud

© Copyright by Michael Persaud 2019

All rights reserved. Without limiting the rights under copyright reserved above, no part of this publication may be reproduced, stored or introduced into a retrieval system, or transmitted, in any form or by any means (electronic, mechanical, photocopying, recording or otherwise), without the proper written permission of the publisher and author of this book, except for the brief quotes in reviews on blogs, websites, essays, newspapers, or magazines.

This book is dedicated to my wife, parents, and siblings, who have always supported me in whatever I choose to do. Special love goes to our cat, Ashleigh, who fills my heart with a lot of love from just looking at his cute face. It is also dedicated to those people who like to explore new cities and countries to enrich their experiences of this world.

Please note: some words in this travel guide may use Canadian spellings in the cases of actual names of places or sites in Canada. They are not typos like in such words as "centre" and "theatre" in place of the American spelling "center" and "theater."

Table of Contents

Welcome to Edmonton!....4

Helpful Hints....7

Average Temperatures....11

Sports Teams....14

Historic Sites....18

Museums & Art Galleries....22

Shopping....29

Festivals and Events....33

Tours....52

Zoo and Parks....57

Accommodations....60

Welcome to Edmonton!

Edmonton is one the great cities of the Prairie provinces which lies in the province of Alberta and in Western Canada. It has the largest indoor shopping mall in the world, which is the West Edmonton Mall. This specific mall also has a skating rink for you to do some spins around the rink.

It's the second largest city in Alberta and just so happens to also be the capital city of this gorgeous province. Its population sits at just over 1 million souls. The only other city larger than Edmonton in Alberta is Calgary, home to the Calgary Stampede.

Edmonton officially became a town on January 9, 1902 and then was incorporated into a full-fledged city in October 8, 1904.

Edmontonians are very nice and hospital people. They are very welcoming and easy to speak to whenever you're visiting. The city, itself, is the most northerly of all the big cities in North America.

The ethnic make-up of the city is comprised of 56% people of European ancestry such as English, French, German, Ukrainian, Scottish and Polish. The main language spoken in Edmonton is English. Of course, French is Canada's second official language. The second largest ethnic groups are comprised of East and Southeast Asians (Chinese, Filipino, and Vietnamese) followed by people of South Asian ancestry. There are, however, peoples of African, South American, Caribbean, and Latin American origins who also call Edmonton home.

Edmonton is known for its plethora of festivals, attractions, museums, and nightlife. That's not to discount some of its sports teams as you will find some rabid hockey and football fans in this town as well.

During your stay in Edmonton do as much as you can to reap the benefits of this wonderful and thoroughly engaging city. It's one of the jewels in the crown of Canada.

Helpful Hints

1. If you will be flying into the Edmonton by airplane it has one major airport which is called the Edmonton International Airport. Its airport code is YEG. All flights from international, national, continental flights from the United States fly into this airport. It is approximately about 30 minutes from down. It is serviced by taxi and the Sky Shuttle. The latter must be booked in advance by calling 1-780-465-8515. You may also wish to rent a car. Some of the most commonly used rental car services are Avis (1-800-879-2847), Alamo (1-800-992-9823), Budget (1-800-661-7027), Hertz (1-800-263-0600) and National (1-800-327-2501). All of the preceding numbers are toll-free when dialed within North America but not from Europe.
2. Via Rail – the national rail service in Canada – also serves Edmonton. The Via Rail station is located at 123600 – 121 St. The American national service Amtrak does not cross the border into Edmonton. If you're coming from Vancouver, Winnipeg, Saskatoon, or Toronto it is possible to take a Via Rail train from those locations into Edmonton. Its website is **www.viarail.ca**. If

you elect to call them their agents are very helpful as well.
3. If you will be coming by way of bus you will end up at the Red Arrow Terminal (**www.redarrow.ca**) which is located in the heart of downtown at 10014 – 104 St. and 5116 Gateway Blvd.
4. If you will be driving into Edmonton there is a distracted driving law which is in effect so no texting, drinking, reading, putting on makeup, eating, fiddling with your GPS, or using your cellphone while driving is an offence.
5. If you will be driving to Edmonton, this wonderful city is located on the QE2, which runs from north to south, and also on the Trans-Canada Yellowhead Highway which runs from east to west.
6. A person must be at least 18 years of age to buy or consume alcohol in the province of Alberta (where Edmonton is located). That same minimum age also applies to people wishing to consume or purchase cannabis which is legal in Canada. Operating a motor vehicle while under the influence alcohol and/or cannabis is against the law.
7. For foreign travelers, Canada does not have a one dollar or two- dollar bill. The smallest denomination of a dollar bill they have is a five-dollar bill. They do have a one-dollar coin called the "loonie" because it has a loon on it and is gold in color. They also

have a two-dollar coin which is silver with a gold center, which is referred to as a "toonie." Their dollar bills are polymer or plastic and they no longer produce paper bills although there are very minimal ones still in circulation which are still legal tender. Canada also does not produce pennies (one cent coins). When making a purchase by credit card or by cash your bill will be rounded up or down to the nearest nickel (5 cents).

Average Temperatures

Edmonton has a moderate climate. It is not inundated with overwhelming snowfall or precipitation like other Canadian cities like Toronto and Montreal. And it does not receive a great deal of rainfall like Vancouver. Keep in mind, with the climate change, like most parts of Canada the weather can be unpredictable. The winters are not excessively harsh and neither is it scorching during the summer months. But always pack for the unexpected because in our current state of affairs when it comes to the weather, anything can happen. Below are the average temperatures and precipitation you can expect:

Month	**Temperature**	**Snow/Rain**
January	-18/9.8 C	21 cm
February	-10.4/-0.3 C	9 cm
March	7.9/0.8 C	26 cm
April	-0.3/10.8 C	12 cm
May	5.2/16 C	8 cm
June	9.6/19.7 C	0 cm
July	12.2/22.5 C	0 cm
August	11.7/22.9 C	0 cm

Month	Temperature	Snow/Rain
September	6.3/16.9 C	0 cm
October	0.3/10.2 C	6 cm
November	-7.8/-0.2 C	22 cm
December	-12.9/-4.5 C	12 cm

Sports Teams

Edmonton has a rich sporting tradition. It does not have a National Football League (NFL) team but it does have it own professional football team which plays in the Canadian Football League (CFL). It also does not have a Major League Baseball (MLB) team but does have a good hockey team which has not faired that well during the last few seasons. That would be the Edmonton Oilers in the National Hockey League (NHL).

Edmonton Oilers – Rogers Place – 102 St. & 104 Ave. --www.oilers.nhl.com

The Edmonton Oilers is one of the storied Canadian hockey teams in the National Hockey League (NHL). They were first in the World Hockey Association (WHA) when they drafted the best hockey player of all time, Wayne Gretzky. When the NWA merged with the NHL, the Edmonton Oilers brought Wayne Gretzky's talents to the masses in North America. With the likes of Gretzky, Mark Messier, and Grant Fuhr, the Edmonton Oilers won several Stanley Cups before Gretzky was traded. Fittingly, there is a Wayne Gretzky statue outside the arena. Now, they have a great franchise player in Connor McDavid. Games are always filled with action and are great to watch the talents of McDavid and his teammates. If you're ever in town during the NHL season, grab a ticket, and you'll have a great time.

Edmonton Eskimos – Commonwealth Stadium – 11000 Stadium Rd. – www.esks.com

The Edmonton Eskimos are one of the most successful Canadian Football League (CFL) professional football teams in Canada. Games are always full of action. CFL rules differ slightly than NFL rules but Eskimos' games will still provide the same level of enjoyment, action, and excitement. Be sure to get your ticket if you'll be in town in the summer and early fall.

Edmonton Stingers – Edmonton EXPO Centre – www.thestingers.ca

Edmonton does not have a National Basketball League (NBA) or D-League franchise team. But they still offer some great action when it comes to having great basketball players. The Edmonton Stingers will still provide the same action and fast-paced level of play. Grab your ticket and get ready for some dunks, awesome lay-ups, or skilled 3-point shooting!

Edmonton Oil Kings – Rogers Place – 102 St. & 104 Ave. – www.oilkings.ca

The Edmonton Oil Kings play in the World Hockey League (WHL) are greatly skilled hockey players. They are so good they garnered the Memorial Cup in 2014, which is quite an accomplishment. You will see some great scoring, slapshots, dekes, and skilled skating just like you would see in the NHL. Get your ticket for a game and sit back for some amazing hockey!

FC Edmonton – Clarke Stadium – 11000 Stadium Rd. – www.fcedmonton.canpl.ca

If you love soccer you will love watching the FC Edmonton during a game. These players are greatly skilled and can produce some wonderful plays and action. They don't play in the Major League Soccer (MLS) but in the Canadian Premier League. Still they will not be outdone and provide some excellent level of play.

Edmonton Prospects – RE/MAX Field – 10223 – 96 Ave. – www.prospectsbaseballclub.com

Take me out to the ball game! The Edmonton Prospects play out of the Western Major Baseball League and have a great roster of players. They are so skilled you will be impressed by how they bat, catch, throw, and maybe even hit home runs. These young men are very impressive to watch in action. If you're in town during their season grab tickets and just sit back for some wonderful baseball!

Historic Sites

To really grasp, or get a good impression of what a city really means, from where it came from during its early beginnings, to the present day it would behoove any visitor to take in some historic sites. Historic sites afford a person to be educated and learn more about a city, what it means to live in that city, and how it evolved from its very inception. Below are some wonderful historic sites that you may consider putting on your itinerary:

Princess Theatre – 10337 Whyte Ave.

Build in the Classical Revival style of architecture, the Princess Theatre featured the earliest movies that were shown. Back then they were called "moving pictures" as this art form, or cinematic displays, were in their infancy. The theater also hosted some vaudeville shows during its early years as that was all the rage back then. This building is the brainchild of architects Wilson and Herrald and is composed of three storeys being erected in 1914. In its present incarnation it is more of an arthouse cinema, with the main theater sitting on the main level, and the smaller more intimate theater situated in the basement.

Fairmont Hotel Macdonald – 10065 – 100 St.

This beautiful hotel was originally built at the turn of the last century in 1915 and is reflective of the Scottish Baronial/ French Chateau architecture movement. In 1983, the hotel became rather decrepit and not being kept to standard, therefore, it almost met the fate of meeting with the wrecking ball. Fortunately, it was saved from being destroyed. It was then designated as an historic site and was fully restored. The hotel itself was originally the railway hotel which was the accommodations for the Grand Trunk Pacific Railway. Its present glory brings back the eyes and mind to its glory past.

McLeod Building – 10134 – 100 St.

Originally constructed in 1915, it was a very innovative architectural structure at the time. The building was the first of its kind which showed what emerging technologies of construction using steel frames could do to bolster the tall skyscrapers at the time. The architectural style it promotes is Chicago commercial which is indicative of buildings which were being erected in The Windy City south of the border.

McKay Ave. School – 10425 – 99 Ave.

The McKay Ave. School was designed and constructed in the Richardson Romanesque style of architecture. It was built in 1905 around the turn of the last century. This school is where the first two sessions of Alberta's legislature had its sittings. It is also in this very structure where Edmonton was recognized and declared a city. In present day it is being used as a repository for the Edmonton Public Schools Archives and Museum. Paying a visit to it will enlighten your mind as to what a great city Edmonton was from its early beginnings.

Museums & Art Galleries

Museums are the lifeblood of any city as it permits patrons to enjoy and become immersed in the very culture that makes a city grow and thrive. It also permits any visitor to see the great artifacts or creations which sustain any city or culture throughout the decades. It would be beneficial to at least take in some museums while you're in the city of Edmonton.

TELUS World of Science – 11211 – 142 St. – www.twoseca

This is a fabulous museum for the curious or those who like to learn new things based in the world of science. It boasts five permanent galleries to keep your mind engaged with some neat and novel exhibits. For the younger set there is a CuriousCITY gallery which is very interactive for kids 8 years of age and under which is totally hands-on. There are daily fascinating demonstrations to brighten your mind; a wonderful IMAX theatre to give you an out of this world experience with some really amazing films; and a planetarium to also experience the vast worlds around us.

Alberta Railway Museum – 24215 – 34 St. – www.albertarailwaymuseum.com

This is by far the largest railway museum you will find in the entire province of Alberta. It offers visitors the chance to see over 75 cars and trains and affords you the opportunity take a ride in one of the locomotives or some the amazing vintage cars on display. It gives a great view into how you see these great means of transportation work and their origins. You also get a sneak peek into the provenance of the Canadian National Railway and the Northern Alberta Railway systems. You are also permitted to touch and feel the vehicles which will only add to your awesome experience.

Alberta Aviation Museum – 11410 Kingsway – www.albertaaviationmuseum.com

This wonderful museum lets you experience aviation in terms of how important it has been for the city of Edmonton, and what it means to citizens. There are many interactive exhibits and static displays to give you a more intimate feel of Edmonton's aviation history. It features in excess of 30 aircrafts, 40 exhibits, and memorabilia to give you an all-encompassing experience. Definitely a must-see for visitors.

Multicultural Heritage Centre – 5411 – 51 St., Stony Plain – www.multicentre.org

This center is situated in the Old Brick School, it was the first high school for Stony Plain dating back to 1925. This building now houses a wonderful art gallery, a great museum, a tasty pie shop, and the Homesteader's Kitchen which affords you the excellent opportunity to delve into some great meals should your tummy be tempted. You peruse the wonderful art in the gallery to get a good impression of what life was like for the initial settlers of the region. It's a very interesting view into the past when life was much more simple.

Reynolds-Alberta Museum – 6426 40 Ave. – www.reynoldsalbertamuseum.com

This excellent museum invites you into Alberta's past to let you see what the cars in the days of yore were like and how people got around. It's the largest collection of cars and airplanes in the entire province. You will get to see horse-drawn carriages – the first means of transportation – to the first cars which were made available. Now this a real treat: you can also be chauffeured around in a vintage car to make you feel like a King or Queen. To get an even better feel you can partake of their 1950's drive-in cinema where you can gaze at some old movies of that period while being firmly ensconced in a vintage car. Now isn't that fabulous?!

Ukrainian Cultural Heritage Village – Yellowhead Highway (Hwy. 16) – www.ukrainianvillage.ca

This cultural center generally covers the period from 1892 to 1930 when the first Ukrainian settlers were first coming to the region. It tells their story in a very vivid and interesting way. Costumed actors play the roles of early settlers recreating the lives of the early settlers to give visitors a very authentic feel to that period in time. There are over 30 fully restored buildings which really evoke that historical moment of the province. It is situated just under 30 minutes east of the city of Edmonton on Yellowhead Highway (Hwy. 16).

Fort Heritage Precinct – 10006 – 100 Ave. – www.fortsask.ca

This historical site lets visitors into the very important and edifying historical period of Fort Saskatchewan North West Mounted Police which dates back to 1875. It is comprised of 8 heritage buildings which are juxtaposed to the very impressive North Saskatchewan River. It is worth paying a visit as this will enable you to really experience what life was like two centuries ago.

Father Lacombe Chapel – 2 St. Vital Ave. – www.history.alberta.ca/fatherlacombe

This is the oldest building in Alberta which was initially constructed in 1861 when the early Métis had come to the province. Religion was usually the centerpiece back in those bygone days and this chapel was erected by Father Lacombe for the largely French-speaking Métis. There will be very informative guides who will provide narrative of what the chapel meant and its importance during the time period. The Métis, for those not aware, were descendants of French and First Nations (what we use to be referred to as Native Indians). You are also permitted to tour the grounds and the cemetery which is where Father Lacombe's final resting place is. Tours are also offered in both English and French.

Royal Alberta Museum – 9810 – 103a Ave. – www.royalalbertamuseum.ca

This is the largest museum in all of Alberta with an immense exhibit space of over 80,000 square feet of exhibits. It has great Natural and History halls as well as a very interesting live Bug Gallery. For the little ones there is a very interactive Children's Gallery to keep them entertained.

Art Gallery of Alberta – 2 Sir Winston Churchill Square -- www.youraga.ca

This art gallery features works of Indigenous artists as they are a very important segment of the art world in Canada. The exhibits feature works Inuit, First Nations, and Métis artists.

Bearclaw Gallery – www.bearclawgallery.com

This is another gallery which celebrates the very important works of Canada's Indigenous artists from the Métis, Inuit, and First Nations. You will see the intricacies and meticulousness these artists employ to create their great works of sculptures, paintings, carvings, crafts, and jewellery. You can also purchase some to take back home with you as a memento of your visit to Edmonton.

Shopping

When you're visiting a city, especially one so nice as Edmonton, you probably want to immerse yourself in the sights and senses, and partake of a little shopping. Yes, of course, you want to purchase some things for yourself, but you may also wish to make some purchases for those people who make your life special and more meaningful. Those family and friends who add true verve and luster to your existence in this world. There are a lot of options in Edmonton where you can exercise your purchasing power. Here are some excellent choices:

West Edmonton Mall – 8882 – 170 St. – www.wem.ca

This is the largest mall in the world covering over 48 city blocks and about 5.3 million square feet of awesome shopping space. Impressively there are over 800 stores and services, in excessive of 100 restaurants, the largest indoor amusement park in the world, world-class attractions, an indoor skating rink, and 5-acre water park. What more could you ask for?! There is also a hotel on site called the Fantasyland Hotel, Europa Boulevard which is a stretch of boutiques, a New Orleans-inspired avenue called fittingly Bourbon Street, the Starlight Casino which has 768 slots, 32 gaming tables, private salons, and 6 restaurants, plus

Halley's Club a supper club which has a cabaret feel to it. Wait! There's more! They also have movie theaters for you to get your movie fix.

South Edmonton Common – 19 Ave. and 99 St. – www.southedmontoncommon.com

This shopping mall is very expansive in size and is home to the Edmonton's only IKEA location. It boasts many outlet stores and several restaurants, just the place where you would like to spend the day. It also features the first Rec Room in Canada.

Edmonton City Centre – 102 Ave. and 102 St. – www.edmontoncitycentre.com

Right in the heart of downtown it can be conveniently accessed by most anyone. CBC Radio calls the Edmonton City Centre home, there are many fashionable stores to choose from, not to mention some great restaurants to dine at, and Landmark Cinemas if you want to catch the latest flick.

Londonderry Mall – 137 Ave. and 66 St. – www.londonderrymall.com

This excellent mall has some great choices for you from their 140 shops and services, refurbished food court which has some great places to please your palate, and a Hudson's Bay to find that special item to accent your wardrobe.

Skyview Power Centre – 13304 – 137 Ave.

A great place to exercise your purchasing power offering some eclectic big box stores such as RW&Co., HomeSense, Reitmans, and Structube. The Skyview Power Centre also has some really wonderful places to dine plus some fantastic coffee shops like Tim Hortons, Starbucks, and Thai Express. A great way to spend the day or the afternoon. Why not pay it a visit?

Manning Town Centre – 37 St. and 153 Ave. – www.manningtowncentre.com

The Manning Town Centre offers some excellent big box stores such as HomeSense, Sport Chek, and Cabela's, plus numerous restaurants and Cineplex Cinemas where you can enjoy the latest movies from Tinseltown. Located in the northeastern portion of Edmonton it also has some great walkways.

Premium Outlet Collection EIA – Outlet Collection Way, Edmonton International Airport – www.premiumoutletcollectioneia.com

Offering more than 100 stores to choose from, this outlet mall is close to Edmonton International Airport. There are many wonderful brand names so there is much to interest you. It also offers an airport shuttle bus, screens to indicate flight times, storage for your luggage, cellphone charging stations, and other services which are just perfect for the ideal shopper in you.

Festivals and Events

The festivals and events offered by any city permits people and visitors to become infused with the many things that make a city more vibrant and very engaging. There are numerous festivals and events put on in Edmonton that does just that, they let you become part of the essential fabric of the city, while at the same time, give you the chance to have a good time. Please check each festival's or event's website for exact dates are they are subject to change without notice, but usually occur in the month where they are indicated.

January

Deep Freeze and Byzantine Winter Festival – www.deepfreezefest.ca

Enjoy the liveliness of winter by immersing yourself in one of the best winter festivals you will find. This festival will let you witness races in actual deep-freezes, such skilled activities as axe throwing, street hockey like you may have enjoyed when growing up, or wagon rides which are always fun for every member of the family.

Ice on Whyte – www.iceonwhyte.ca

This is a very artistic event where you an ooh and aah at what you are seeing. Held at the Old Strathcona you get to see some amazing ice sculptures, listen to some great live music, eat some very delectable foods, and even have the opportunity to descend down a giant ice slide! What more could you ask for?

Flying Canoe Volant Festival – www.flyingcanoevolant.ca

This festival is based on a French legend and occurs after dark. There will be many amazing light installations for you to observe, great live music, some excellent Indigenous art, and also be able to listen to some wonderful storytellers spin their yarns. Great for a night out!

February

Silver Skate Festival – www.silverskatefestival.org

This the city's longest running winter festival. It has something for everyone and for those young or young at heart. There will be eclectic art on display, some great cultural activities, and lots of sporting events to keep you immensely engaged. You will be able to cook bannock over fire, encourage the long-blade speed skaters, and also get to venture into a giant ice castle in Hawrelak Park.

SOUND OFF: A Deaf Theatre Festival – www.soundofffestival.com

Edmonton, and Canada as a whole, are inclusive societies, so it is not surprising that the city would have a festival to promote those who are hearing impaired. The festival focuses on deaf artists in how they express themselves when it comes to the performing arts using American Sign Language (ASL). This might be a new, novel, and thoroughly interesting festival for you to partake of.

March

SkirtsAfire herArts Festival – www.skirtsafire.com

This unique festival celebrates women in the performing arts which give them a new voice and renewed prominence in society. It gives them a platform to express themselves whether it be in music, in film, as dancers, actors, or writers. This is something we need more of as it is not only empowering to women but it permits attendees to see the world in a whole new light.

April

Edmonton Poetry Festival – www.edmontonpoetryfestival.com

Poetry is a style of writing which lets you see into the heart and soul of the writer, whether their style is cryptic, free verse, avant-garde, haiku, or what have you. This festival celebrates poets and their varied creative works. You will also be treated to live music, some excellent readings, get to converse with some very inspiring poets, and get a chance to even write a poem using your own imagination and life experience.

Rubaboo Arts Festival – www.albertaaboriginalarts.ca

Experiencing Indigenous culture always adds another dimension to our world. This is the only festival in Alberta which gives you an opportunity to delve into Indigenous art, food, music, dance, theater, and permit you to also do some very interesting workshops.

May

Northwestfest – www.northwestfest.ca

This film festival is based in reality as all films featured here have to deal with a topic which is nonfiction and has a great deal of relevance to our society or our world. Some of the topics concern social and environmental causes (which is of great concern today), the prevailing topic of human rights, and the enduring capacity to survive beyond all odds.

Rainmaker Rodeo and Exhibition – www.rainmaker.ab.ca

Yee-ha! Feel your inner cowboy or cowgirl, as you might need a ten- gallon hat for this festival but not really. You get to enjoy some exciting midway rides, a very thrilling parade, a market where you might find that special item to spice up your life, activities for the entire family, the always amazing rodeo, and live music to let you sit back and hear some great tunes.

International Children's Festival of the Arts – www.childfest.com

If there is a child in your life, or you just feel very young (after all, age is just a number), this is a great festival to partake of some very great storytellers, inspiring musicians, skilled dancers, and not to be missed puppeteers. And, yes, there is more, you also have the chance of hearing some great music, engaging in creating some wonderful crafts, participate in games, and experience the wit of performers. You will most certainly have a memorable time.

NextFest – www.nextfest.org

This very important festival celebrates young talent and their emerging skills in the world of arts. Watch and experience young people showcase their gifts in such things as dance, music, art, the world of film, express themselves in writing, performing, and of course see their inspirations via the fashions they create.

Edmonton Craft Beer Festival – www.albertabeerfestivals.com

If you need to wet your whistle, this is the perfect festival for you. You will get the chance to sample some of your old favorites and also try some 300 different brews produced by 70 breweries. There will also be many workshops to teach you more about the brews so you can be educated of their provenance and what makes them so great and fulfilling.

June

Edmonton Pride Festival – www.edmontonpride.ca

The LGBTQ community is an important part of any society. They populate many professions that comprise a city from the arts, to medicine, to writing, finance, or any others that make a city complete and whole. The Edmonton Pride Festival celebrates this thriving community with many parties, a street festival, and also in the performing arts. Come join the festivities and partake of some fun and good times. Please check the website for specific dates.

Improvaganza – www.rapidfiretheatre.com

Come and be prepared to laugh your pants off. This event promotes improvisational comedy with many comedic performers who will have you laughing in the aisles. It's Canada's largest improv comedy festival with performers hailing from across the entire country. There will be some improv competitions as well as some entertaining workshops.

Porkapalooza BBQ Festival – www.porkapalooza.ca

Are you a carnivore? This festival is perfect for you and your palate. It has everything you will love if you're a connoisseur of BBQ who loves to indulge in meat. There will be food trucks on hand for you to delve into some great eats and live music to please your ears. There will also be a champion at the end of all the good times as to who is the best grill master.

Freewill Shakespeare Festival – www.freewillshakespeare.com

William Shakespeare is arguably the best playwright who ever lived. His themes span every emotion known to humans. There are tragedies, love stories, dramas, and comedy which make up his plays. This festival celebrates his very important works which have graced humanity for over a century. Please check the website to see what plays are being offered this year to edify your intellectual mind and soul. The venue is Hawrelak Park.

The Works Art and Design Festival – www.theworks.ab.ca

If you're an art lover or just love to immerse your mind in the creative arts, this is the perfect festival for you. There will be tons of arts on display, artists creating their works, a bustling street market, live music, and more to engage you and keep you interested in the world of art.

Edmonton International Jazz Festival – www.edmontonjazz.com

Music soothes the savage beast. It puts us in a different mindset, one that is more placid and one that feels lost in the depths of good tunes. Jazz is a genre of music which makes us feel more attuned to the musicians because jazz is such a pacifying force. This festival celebrates jazz musicians who come from all corners of the globe to entertain you with their great renditions or their own original music.

Sand on Whyte – www.sandonwhyteca

In the winter there are ice sculptures. So, in the summer fittingly there are sand sculptures. In this event you will see some of the most creative and innovative sand sculptures to meet the eye. You can observe the artists work on their larger than life creations on Whyte Avenue.

July

Canada Day Celebrations – www.edmonton.ca

Canada is one of the greatest nations on the earth. It recognizes diversity in its population, respects the rights of women, and marginalized groups. July 1st marks the day of Canada's confederation as a country. There will be a parade, tons of activities, and myriad fireworks to celebrate the nation's birthday. You will feel left out if you do not partake of the many activities to celebrate this very special day. It's fun for the entire family! For those not in the know, the momentous day is also called Canada Day.

Historic Festival and Doors Open Edmonton – www.historicedmonton.ca

This festival is a wonderful opportunity to experience the city's many historic sites and museums. You will also get to take some nifty streetcar rides, participate in some very immersive activities, hop on a horse drawn carriage, and listen to some great orators tell some amazing stories to brighten your mind.

Whyte Avenue Art Walk – www.art-walk.ca

Whyte Avenue is the place to be where you can see the works of some excellent artists. It's rather akin to a large canvas but with many diverse works. It takes place for three entire days so you have ample time to peruse the art works. Please check the website for dates.

Edmonton International Street Performers Festival – www.edmontonstreetfest.com

There are some amazing amateur performers who ply their trade but are not household names. This festival celebrates them in all their grandeur. It lasts for just over a week and lets you become entertained in many fields of entertainment like comedy, puppets, magic, juggling, music, and other genres. This is a great time for one and all! Please check the website for dates and times. This is similar to busker festivals in other major cities.

Africanival – www.africanival.org

Africa has its own distinctive culture with many important and very relevant artists. This festival gives you a chance to become not only privy to some great performances but some delicious Caribbean foods, a very enticing parade, so much more to add more niceties to your summer. Please check their website for dates.

Taste of Edmonton – www.tasteofedm.ca

Are you a foodie or just really, really like delicious food? The Taste of Edmonton lets you enjoy some great cuisine from some of the city's best restaurant. It's a white tent affair where participants get to indulge in some pre-set menus including some great beverages, performers, and some great live music. What more could you ask for?

Edmonton Carnaval – www.edmontoncarnaval.com

Edmonton is a thriving city with a great Latin America community. New Orleans has Mardi Gras and Trinidad & Tobago has Carnival, Edmonton has Carnaval. This fabulous festival gives people the opportunity to experience Latin American culture, music, and, of course, some amazing food! Please check their website for exact dates.

K-Days – www.k-days.com

It's not surprising that Edmonton is known as a city of festivals. K-Days has more to entertain you and to engage your senses with some great sites and sounds. There will be a midway, a wonderful parade, lots of live entertainment, specialty foods, and fireworks to grace the night's sky.

Interstellar Rodeo – www.interstellarrodeo.com

This three-day festival opens your mind to some eclectic brands of music including blues, country, folk, gospel, bluegrass, and rock. It has something for everyone whether you like your music more mellow or with a bit of edge. All the amazing music will be staged on Hawrelak Park Heritage Amphitheatre.

August

Edmonton Heritage Festival – www.heritagefest.ca

To usher in the last month of summer, Edmonton offers its heritage festival. There is still time to enjoy some great music, tons of great cuisine from around the world, some excellent musical performances, dancers galore, arts and crafts displays, and some very exotic cultural offerings.

Edmonton Folk Music Festival – www.edmontonfolkfest.org

This is another great music festival that gives you a wonderful chance to hear magnificent blues, folk, bluegrass, and gospel performers. All the fun takes place at Gallagher Park on a hillside. It's a fabulous outdoor venue which pits you with terrific music and being outdoors in the elements.

Cariwest Caribbean Arts Festival – www.cariwest.ca

One of the best Caribbean festivals in all of Canada, it lets you become embroiled in an extravagant parade, exciting parties, brilliant costumes reminiscent of the Caribbean cultural heritage, soca and calypso music, and steel-pan music. And, yes, there will be some great dancers too who know how to whine (in West Indian parlance, that means how to swivel their hips).

Edmonton International Fringe Theatre Festival – www.fringetheatre.ca

One of the largest fringe theater festivals in the world, it features some amazing and innovative artists the likes of which will provide great and very affordable performances. These performers hail from North America and throughout the world. There will be over 1,200 acts in more than 50 venues to entertain you. Please check their website for dates and show times.

Edmonton Rock Music Festival – www.edmontonrockfest.com

Get ready to shake your money maker to some of those iconic rock acts you will see at this great festival celebrating rock music. All the action is at Hawrelak Park. It takes place over a weekend in August so please consult their website for the exact dates and show times.

**Edmonton Dragon Boat Festival –
www.edmontondragonboatfestival.ca**

The Chinese-Canadian community is one of the most important in the quilt of Canada. In Edmonton there is a thriving Chinese community. The dragon boat festival lets you take in some skilled athletes as they compete to see who is the best in this very exciting competition. Come and join in on the fun.

**Edmonton Blues Festival –
www.bluesinternationalltd.com**

From the deep south of the United States was germinated the blues which originated with such black singers as Muddy Waters, Robert Johnson, and B.B. King. The music went on to influence bands like Led Zeppelin, The Rolling Stones, and The Beatles. It continues to evolve and this festival offers both acoustic acts as well as electric guitar acts ranking from the funk to blues to zydeco.

**Symphony Under the Sky –
www.winspearcentre.com**

This music festival is celebrated in the great outdoors offering classical music, more contemporary fare, and even some soundtracks from the great films of Hollywood. There is something for everyone so good time is in store for all.

September

Kaleido Family Arts Family – www.kaleidofest.ca

Perfect for the entire family this wonderful festival has something for everyone. There will be interesting readings, live entertainment, enticing films, amazing dancers, and plays to keep you engaged and thoroughly entertained. Plus, you will have the chance to shop for some great products as well as view some nice art displays.

Edmonton International Film Festival – www.edmontonfilmfest.com

All over the world there are very inviting film festivals like Cannes in France, Telluride, Sundance, and the New York Film Festival in the United States, and the Toronto International Film Festival in Toronto. Well, not to be outdone, Edmonton has a great film festival of its own. This festival however focuses on independent films. There will be many films screened with a chance for attendees to meet filmmakers and stars as well. The movies come across the world so you are in for a real treat!

October

Edmonton Comedy Festival – www.atbcomedy.com

If you want your funny bone tickled this is the festival for you. It promotes and celebrates funny men and women from all over North America and their brand of humor. It's a laugh-a-minute joy ride for all those who take in these shows!

LitFest: Edmonton's Nonfiction Festival – www.litfestalberta.com

This is the largest festival of its kind devoted to works of nonfiction by some very inspiring authors. Their will be a lot of discussions and readings to keep your mind stimulated by writers from Canada and around the world. It will be accented by some great wines, excellent food, and live music.

November

Farmfair International – www.farmfairinterntional.com

This fair is for those selling livestock or just to have them on display. These animals are beautiful to look at and the event is the largest of its kind in all of Canada. There is the RAM Marketplace which is perfect to go shopping and amidst all the bustling crowds there will be live entertainment, competitions, a rodeo, and some demonstrations to really enlighten your mind.

Edmonton Rocky Mountain Wine and Food Festival – www.rockymountainwine.com

For the gourmand and wine connoisseur in you, there is this festival which will tantalize your taste buds. There will be some amazing foods for those who appreciate gourmet foods as well as some great beverages when it comes to wine, beer, scotch, and other alcoholic beverages. You don't have to be a sommelier to appreciate the taste of good wine and beer. But we're sure you already knew that! Bring your appetite!

Festival of Trees – www.festivaloftrees.ab.ca

Just on the cusp of Christmas here is the perfect festival to usher in Santa's season. There will be many wonderfully decorated trees on display, some deliciously decorated cakes, and of course, some nice gingerbread houses which will infuse your soul with the spirit of Christmas. There will be the added bonus of scavenger hunts for the entire family, not to mention some great live entertainment, and a special visit from the Jolly Old Elf himself.

December

Zoominescence: A Festival of Light – www.buildingourzoo.com

Here is a festival that is sure to really light up your life! Walk through the zoo with a delicious hot chocolate and enjoy the myriad brilliant lights on display by some artists from Edmonton. It takes place every weekend in the month of December.

Tours

Edmonton has some wonderful tours to let you enjoy the city to its fullest. There are many tours to choose from whether be a historic tour, a foodie tour, a walking tour, or just a scenic tour to open your eyes to the great city you are visiting. Below are some stellar options you could make use of.

Foodie Tours

Edmonton Food Tours – www.abertafoodtours.ca

This tour will really stir the foodie in you. You will stop at some of the most recognized spots in Edmonton at such dining options in the downtown core as delicious bakeries, or a farmers' market. And there's more – you will be able to be engaged in a cooking class as well. What more could you ask for?

Edmonton Brewery Tours – www.edmontonbrewerytours.ca

Edmonton is a world class city and its brewery tours shows it's always at the forefront of what is happening in the world of beverages. You will get to tour breweries and distilleries and hear some tantalizing stories while also indulging in some delicious samples.

Urban Pedal Tours – www.urbanpedaltours.com

This bicycle tour is perfect for those who like to feel the wind against their faces while also traversing the city on two wheels. You will be afforded the great opportunity to also visit some brewpubs in Old Strathcona and learn more about this thriving scene in Alberta's second largest city.

Scenic Tours

Segway Adventure Tours

Almost every large city has a Segway tour. They let you not only master a new skill by learning how to ride on a Segway but give you an awesome chance to see the city in the process. Prior to the tour you are taught how to use a Segway and then you're off to take in some wonderful parkland areas. Tours are offered all year long.

E-Bike Tours – www.revolutioncycle.com

These tours let you become acquainted with new technology as you ride with electric bicycles. This tour is the first of its kind in Canada. You have the option of choosing a 2-hour tour or the longer more immersive 5-hour tour. Since your pedaling is electric-assisted it will not be as trying as using a regular bicycle giving you more time to enjoy what you're seeing.

Big E Bus Tours – www.edmontontours.com

This tour lets you board a bus to let you learn more about how Edmonton is run as a city and its many industries plus the people who work in those industries. You can also opt for the tour of the Ukrainian Village & Elk Island Tour to get a new perspective of the city.

Walking Tour

Ghost Tours – www.edmontonghosttours.com

Have you ever seen a ghost or spirit? Don't be afraid, as this 80-minute tour will take you through Old Strathcona and the University of Alberta to enlighten you as to where ghosts or apparitions may have been possibly scene. Dress comfortably and bring your walking shoes as this tour is mainly outdoors.

Historic Walking Tours

Fairmont Hotel Macdonald – 10065 – 100 St. -- www.fairmont.com/macdonald

This is one of the gems of the city being around since the early days of Edmonton when it was a railway hotel which was then turned into a luxury property. Sip some delicious afternoon tea and then proceed on a grand tour of this immaculate hotel.

Alberta Legislature – 10800 – 97 Ave. – www.assembly.ab.ca

This is where all spirited political debates take place. Tours are available in both of Canada's official languages English and French. The tour is free and you get to learn not only about the history of the legislature but its great architecture as well.

Rutherford House –11153 Saskatchewan Drive – www.rutherfordhousephs.ca

Rutherford House was once the residence of Alberta's first premier. In Canada a premier is like a state governor in the United States. This fully restored gorgeous Edwardian home offers a free walking tour to let you know more about its importance in the social fabric of Edmonton.

Zoo and Parks

Getting back to a city's nature scene permits visitors to see another aspect of Edmonton. It will let you to not only commune with nature but give you a personal and a more relaxing and intimate view of the city.
Edmonton has one of the best views, when it comes to natural surroundings in Canada, not to mention some of the most gorgeous parks as well.

Edmonton Valley Zoo – 13315 Buena Vista Rd. – www.valleyzoo.ca

The Edmonton Valley Zoo encapsulates visitors with all the very exotic and amazing animals they have on display. It lets you into their world where you can see them more up close and personal. It is open year-round and has some great demonstrations which will thrill your heart. The zoo had over 350 exotic animals, endangered species, fox, seals, and an artic exhibit as well. You will be totally entranced by the polar bears too! They offer a Little Children's Zoo, a café to get a bite to eat, and a souvenir shop where you can purchase some nice keepsakes. Please check their website for admission prices and times.

John Janzen Nature Centre – 7000 – 143 St. – www.edmonton.ca

This center lets you commune with nature as you are permitted to get more engaged and involved with your surroundings in the great outdoors. John Janzen is now deceased, but was a student of agriculture, who worked for the parks department, and played a pivotal role in saving the land from being developed commercially thereby preserving it. There are hands-on programs available for all age groups, nature walks, and exploring all the intricate trails throughout the groups. The center offers great fun for those who are die-hard environmentalists or for anyone who would just like to explore the natural environment the way it was meant to be. Please consult their website for dates, times, and costs.

Elk Island National Park – 35km east of Edmonton on Highway 16 – www.pc.gc.ca

You've probably heard of Algonquin Park in Ontario and Banff National Park in Alberta, well, Edmonton has its own national park in Elk Island. Designated in 1906 its primary focus was to protect the elk population. It has blossomed to also protect 250 species of birds, moose, deer, bison, and many more animals. There are numerous conservation efforts underway in the park but if you're the outdoor adventurer type you can also go canoeing, camping, or hiking. The park is open year-round. Please visit their websites for costs and admission prices.

Accommodations

Wherever you rest your tired head and feet from exploring Edmonton, may not be secondary but, of course, you want to find a good reputable hotel with good services (and maybe a continental or buffet breakfast) just to your liking. Listing all the services of each hotel is beyond the scope of this book because this guide book is not updated every time a service may be added at a hotel. That's why we've provided you with their phone numbers so you can seek them out and see if they are to your liking. You may also wish to google each hotel's website if they appeal to you. Remember if you're booking with a third-party website, and not the hotel's website, you might not have the support services if you need to cancel, or maybe charged a fee, whereas most hotels do not charge a fee for cancelling. Just keep that in mind when using hotel websites which offer you deals. Yes, it's true you may be saving some money, but may not be entitled to after booking service. Also, when you're calling a toll-free number for a hotel (if it's listed on their website, we've provided you with their local number so you can contact them directly), you may not be calling a hotel directly but their central reservations, which may be located in another Canadian city or country (probably the United States). Please consult each hotel's website for amenities and services they offer to see if it might be to your liking and would be suited to your travel needs. Also, with Airbnb please be cognizant you are getting what you see online. Read reviews before booking as you want to be sure your host is reputable and will be easy to deal with. You don't want to end up in a nightmare situation. If continental breakfast is offered that is a true bonus. The hotels below are listed according to what section of the city they are located:

Downtown Edmonton

Chateau Louis Hotel – 11727 Kingsway – 1-780-424-6682 (Upscale)

Best Western Plus City Centre Inn – 11310 – 109 St. – 1-780-479-2042 (Economy)

Courtyard by Marriott – 1 Thornton Court, 99 St. & Jasper Ave. – 1-780-423-9999 (Moderately priced)

Delta Edmonton Centre Suite Hotel – 10222 – St. – 1-780-429-3900 (Upscale)

Fairmont Hotel Macdonald – 10065 – 100 St. – 1-780-424-5181 (Upscale)

Holiday Inn Express Downtown – 10010 – 104 St. – 1-780-423-2450 (Economy)

Sutton Place Hotel – 10235 – 101 St. – 1-780-428-7111 (Upscale)

Comfort Inn & Suites Downtown – 10425 – 100 Ave. – 1-780-423-5611 (Economy)

Westin Edmonton – 10135 – 100 St. – 1-780-426-3636 (Moderately priced)

Coast Edmonton Plaza Hotel – 10155 – 105 St. – 1-780-423-4811 (Moderately priced)

West Edmonton

Comfort Inn West Edmonton – 17610 – 100 Ave. – 1-780-484-4415 (Economy)

Courtyard by Marriott Edmonton West – 10011 – 184 St. – 1-780-638-6070 (Moderately priced)

Coast West Edmonton Hotel and Conference Centre – 18035 Stony Plain Rd. – 1-780-483-7770 (Moderately priced)

Doubletree by Hilton Hotel West Edmonton – 16615 – 109 Ave. – 1-780-484-0821 (Moderately priced)

Quality West Edmonton – 17803 Stony Plain Rd. -- 1-780-484-8000 (Economy)

Travelodge Edmonton West – 18320 Stony Plain Rd. – 1-780-483-6031 (Economy)

Hampton Inn and Suites Edmonton West – 18304 – 100 Ave. – 1-780-484-7280 (Moderately priced)

Sandman Hotel Edmonton West – 17635 Stony Plain Rd. – 1-780-483-1385 (Moderately priced)

Super 8 Edmonton West – 16818 – 118 Ave. – 1-780-455-1111 (Economy)

South Edmonton

Holiday Inn Express South Ellerslie Road – 950 Parsons Rd. SW – 1-780-784-8500 (Economy)

Four Points by Sheraton Edmonton South – 7230 Argyll Rd. – 1-780-465-7931 (Moderately priced)

Days Inn Edmonton South – 10333 – University Ave. – 1-780-430-0011 (Economy)

Best Western Plus South Edmonton Inn and Suites – 1204 –101 St. SW – 1-780-801-3580 (Economy)

Delta Edmonton South Hotel – 4404 Gateway Blvd. – 1-780-434-6415 (Moderately priced)

Super 8 Edmonton South – 3610 Gateway Blvd. – 1-780-433-8688 (Economy)

Four Points by Sheraton Edmonton Gateway – 10010 – 12 Ave. SW – 1-780-801-4000 (Moderately priced)

Radisson Hotel and Convention Centre – 4520 – 76 Ave. – 1-780-468-5400 (Moderately priced)

Airport Area

Days Inn Edmonton Airport – 5705 – 50 St., Leduc, Alberta – 1-780-986-6550 (Economy)

Travelodge Edmonton Airport – 5704 – 50 St., Leduc, Alberta – 1-780-986-2264 (Economy)

Wingate by Wyndham Edmonton Airport – 7120 Sparrow Dr., Leduc, Alberta – 1-780-769-0079 (Moderately priced)

Best Western Plus Denham Inn and Suites – 5207 – 50, Leduc, Alberta – 1-780-986-2241 (Economy)

Quality Inn and Suites Edmonton – 501 – 11 Ave., Nisku, Alberta – 1-780-955-3001 (Economy)

About the author: Michael Persaud is a freelance writer and author. He has also worked in the field of tourism for over two decades and is a certified travel agent. He would like to extend his gratitude to you for purchasing this book. He was a former music critic and reviewer for his college newspaper. He also worked as a restaurant reviewer for a community newspaper. He has written for numerous publications including the largest newspaper in Canada, by circulation, the Toronto Star, The Downsview Advocate, Equality, Afterword, Write Magazine (now defunct – this publication was not affiliated with the Writers' Union of Canada), Eye Weekly (now defunct), and The Outreach Connection. He loves trivia and loves to watch Jeopardy when time permits. If you liked this book you might also like to try one of his other titles:

The Ultimate Trivia Book

Random Facts About Rock Music's Greatest Acts

True Paranormal Stories: Stories You Will Have to Read in Order to Believe

Ottawa Travel Guide

Calgary Travel Guide

How to Win the Lottery!

800 Ultimate Trivia Questions

Ultimate Rock and Roll Trivia

        …. continued

Massive Movie Trivia

Toronto: A Complete Guide on the City

The Beatles

The Amazing Trivia Book

Inspirational Quotes for Every Day of the Year

Viva Morrissey

Adele: Voice of an Angel

Essential New York: A Tourist Guide on the City

How to Make Even More Money: Learning the Tricks That Will Get You Ahead

A Montreal Travel Guide

How to Find a Job in Hard Times

How to Win Friends Easily

How to Save More Money

A Canadian Childhood